The Poetry of Laurence Binyon

Volume V - The Death of Adam & Other Poems

Robert Laurence Binyon, CH, was born on August 10th, 1869 in Lancaster in Lancashire, England to Quaker parents, Frederick Binyon and Mary Dockray.

He studied at St Paul's School, London before enrolling at Trinity College, Oxford, to read classics.

Binyon's first published work was Persephone in 1890. As a poet, his output was not prodigious and, in the main, the volumes he did publish were slim. But his reputation was of the highest order. When the Poet Laureate, Alfred Austin, died in 1913, Binyon was considered alongside Thomas Hardy and Rudyard Kipling for the post which was given to Robert Bridges.

Binyon played a pivotal role in helping to establish the modernist School of poetry and introduced imagist poets such as Ezra Pound, Richard Aldington and H.D. (Hilda Doolittle) to East Asian visual art and literature. Most of his career was spent at The British Museum where he produced many books particularly centering on the art of the Far East.

Moved and shaken by the onset of the World War I and its military tactics of young men slaughtered to hold or gain a few yards of shell-shocked mud Binyon wrote his seminal poem *For the Fallen*. It became an instant classic, turning moments of great loss into a National and human tribute.

After the war, he returned to the British Museum and wrote numerous books on art; especially on William Blake, Persian and Japanese art.

In 1931, his two volume Collected Poems appeared and in 1933, he retired from the British Museum.

Between 1933 and 1943, Binyon published his acclaimed translation of Dante's *Divine Comedy* in an English version of terza rima.

During the Second World War Binyon wrote another poetic masterpiece '*The Burning of the Leaves*', about the London Blitz.

Robert Laurence Binyon died in Dunedin Nursing Home, Bath Road, Reading, on March 10th, 1943 after undergoing an operation.

Index of Contents

DEDICATION

TO C. M. P.

O love in whose heart-murmured name
Is charm against life's endless wrongs
Since all the untuned world became
In you a song!

I bring not only all I wrought
Into the faltering words of speech,
I dedicate the song I sought
Yet could not reach,

Nay, all that passionately fired
My heart with hope for ever new
Of unattained, but deep-desired
Beauty, to you,

16th August, 1903

THE DEATH OF ADAM

Cedars, that high upon the untrodden slopes
Of Lebanon stretch out their stubborn arms,
Through all the tempests of seven hundred years
Fast in their ancient place, where they look down
Over the Syrian plains and faint blue sea.
When snow for three days and three nights hath fallen
Continually, and heaped those terraced boughs
To massy whiteness, still in fortitude
Maintain their aged strength, although they groan;
In such a wintriness of majesty,
O'ersnowed by his uncounted years, and scarce
Supporting that hard load, yet not overcome.
Was Adam: all his knotted thews were shrunk.
Hollow his mighty thighs, toward which his beard.
Pale as the stream of far-seen waterfalls.
Hung motionless; betwixt the shoulders grand
Bowed was the head, and dim the gaze; and both
His heavy hands lay on his marble knees.
So sits he all day long and scarcely stirs,
And scarcely notes the bright shapes of his sons
Moving in the broad light without his tent,
That propt on poles about a giant oak
Looks southward to the river and the vale:
Only sometimes slowly he turns his head,
As seeking to recover some lost thought
From the dear presence of the white-haired Eve
Who, less in strength, hath less endured, and still
With slow and careful footsteps tendeth him,
Or seated opposite with silent eyes
Companions him; their thoughts go hand in hand.
So now she sits reposing in the dusk
Of their wide tent, like a great vision throned
Of the Earth Mother, tranquil and august.
Accorded to some youthful votary
Deep in an Asian grove, under the moon.

Peace also rests on Adam; not such peace
As comes forlornly to men dulled with cares.
Whom no ennobling memory uplifts;
Peace of a power far mightier than his own.
Outlasting all it fostered into life,
Pervades him and sustains him: such a peace
As blesses mossed and mouldering architraves
Of pillars standing few among the wreck
Of many long since fallen, pillars old.
Reared by a race long vanished, where the birds
Nest as in trees, and every crevice flowers.

As mothering Earth, having some time indulged
Men's little uses, makes their ruin fair
Ere in her bosom it be folded up.
Thus Adam's mind relinquishing the world,
That grows more dim around him every day,
Withdraws into itself, and in degree
As all that mates him to the moving hours,
Even as his outward joy and vigour fail.
So surely turns his homing spirit back
Unto those silent sources whence delight
And hope and strength and buoyancy of old
Flowed fresh upon his youth, persisting still
To seek those first and fairest memories
In youth and sunshine O how lightly lost,
How difficult in darkness to regain!
He sits in idle stillness, yet at times
From the dark wells of musing some old hour
Floats upward, as the tender lotus lifts
Her swaying stalk up through the limpid depth
Of pools in rivers never known to man.
And buoyed on idle wet luxurious leaves
Peacefully opens white bloom after bloom.
He is rapt far from this last shore of age;
He sees the face of Eve as she approached
To bring him flowers new-found in Paradise,
Or hiding her young sorrow on his breast;
And Abel as a child and Cain with him
Playing beneath the shadow of old trees,
All dearer by the desert interposed
Of time and toil and passionate regret.
Troubling his inmost spirit, until his face,
Wrought with remembrance and with longing, wears
The pressure and the sign of all that swells
And brims his heart, fain to be freed in speech.

"What ails thee, Adam?" gentle Eve began.
"Why art thou troubled, what thoughts vex thy mind?
For though my eyes are dim, yet I can see
Thy breast heaves upward, and long sighs go forth,
And thou dost move thy hands, and shake thy head.'
But Adam answered not; he seemed alone.
Then, lifting up his eyes, he saw his sons
Slowly approaching in the evening light
With all their flocks; and many voices rose
On the clear air about the tents and trees.
As they made ready for the sacrifice
Before the evening meal: soon they drew near
To Adam's tent; and he looked on them all,

Standing to wait his blessing, of all years.
From the boy Adriel to the aged Seth,
Outlined with glory by the sinking sun.
Strange in their strength and beauty they appeared;
And Adam, though he saw them, seemed to gaze
Beyond them, seeking what he found not there.
Over them all his eyes unresting roved.
While they in silence waited for his word.
At last he spoke: "Where is my first-born Cain?"
They looked on one another. Few had heard
That darkened name; but Eve bowed down her head.
And Seth stood forth amid them hushed and spoke
With a grave utterance, "Cain is far away.
Thou knowest, O my father, how we have heard
That far beyond the mountains to the east
He dwells, and ever wanders o'er that land.
Many days' journey must a man be gone
Ere he reach thither and return again;
Nor know we certainly where Cain may dwell.
Yet what thou biddest, that shall be performed;
Shall we send to him?" Adam answered, "Send:
Let them go quickly, see that they make haste.
But on the tenth day bid them come again,
Whether they have found him, or have found him not.
For mine eyes fail, yea, and my heart grows cold."

Heavy as pale clouds of October roll
Over the soaring snows of Ararat,
The vapour of oblivion fell once more
Down over Adam's head, in languor drooped
Between his mighty shoulders on his breast.
From morn to night, from night to morn he sat
As in a trance of deep thought undivined.
His children looking on his face were filled
With desolation and disquietude,
Sad as Armenian shepherds when they watch
For the still clouds to roll from those great peaks.
Praying the clear bright North winds to restore
Their guardian mountain; with such heavy hearts
They waited for his face to give a sign
That still gave none. Listless amid their toil
They grew, and sitting idle by their flocks
Each from his station, scattered on the hills,
Turned often to the east, in hope to spy
The messengers returning: but at eve
While the grey-bearded elders patient sat
In the cool tent-doors, they would pace the shore
Under the gathering stars, and murmured low

One to another saying, "What is this
That comes upon us all, what evil thing
Whereof we have not heard? What cloud is fallen
Upon our father Adam, and why seeks he
This Cain whose name we know not? Peace is gone,
And nothing now is as it was before,"
And others answered, "Well for us, if they
Whom we have sent on such a hazard come
Ever again or we behold them more!
Would they had never gone on this dark quest!
We have no hunters brave and swift as they, —
Ophir, that was the strongest of us all.
And Iddo, that could match the eagle's sight."
Thus the young men spoke their despondent mind.
But every morn renewing wearied hope
They turned with the sun rising to the east.
And numbered the long hours till noon, and still
Nor morn nor noon brought tidings; and each eve
Watching tall herons by the sandy pools
Widen their wings and slow with trailing feet
And lifted head sail off into the sky.
They followed them with long and silent thoughts
Over the darkening mountains, far and far
Into that never yet imagined world
Beginning to oppress them; whither now
Their fears went wandering through enormous night
Thus waxed and waned each heavy day; at last
From mouth to mouth the unquiet murmur ran,
"Tis the ninth evening, and they are not come!"

The kingly star had stolen from his throne
In the first brightening of the morrow morn:
And far in the east, with frail cloud overspread.
Light hovered in the pale immensity.
A mile-broad shade beneath the mountain slept;
But opposite a dewy glimmer soon
Moulded the shapes of rough crags, and beneath
Strewn boulders, and thin streams, and slopes obscure.
There, on the slopes amid the rocks appeared
The youth of Adam's race, assembled forms
Sitting or standing with hand-shaded eyes
At gaze into the eastern gorge, where hills
Between dark shoulders inaccessible
Opened a narrowing way into the dawn.
Stiller than statues, yet with beating hearts
They waited while the wished light kindled clear,
Invading that deep valley, until the sun
Flamed warm upon their limbs through coloured air.

And slow rose upward: it was nigh to noon:
At last a motion on the horizon stirred
And a faint dust in the far gorge was blown.
Then those that sat rose up and gazed erect,
And those that stood moved and stept on a pace.
And as they watched amid the shining dust
Two far-off forms appeared, but only two.
Their straining eyes watched, but no other came.
A sigh ran through their troubled ranks, they turned
To one another, then again to those
Two lonely journeyers downcast and slow.
Who now discerned them from afar and raised
Their hands in greeting; then some ran, with cakes
Of bread, and skins of milk, and honeycomb^,
Down the great slope to meet the messengers;
And others climbed the ridge and backward ran
Down to the tents, the river, and the vale.
And came to where Seth sat beneath a tree
Waiting, with folded arms, and cried to him,
"They come, they come; but Cain comes not with them."
Then Seth arose and came to Adam's tent.
And stood before his father in the door.
Eve questioning sought his eyes: he shook his head
And looked on Adam; motionless he sat
Plunged in a trance, yet dimly was aware
Of tidings, as he heard the voice of Seth,
"'Tis the tenth morning, and thy sons return."
Faintly by imperceptible degrees
Light stole o'er Adam's features, and Seth saw
The wellings of his troubled mind on them,
As one who in a cavern lifts a torch
And sees the gradual recesses grow
Out of their ancient gloom, uncertain shapes
Of rugged roof and walls without an end:
So dark from innermost obscurity
The slumbrous memories of Adam rose
And on his face appeared: yet still a veil
Remained betwixt his senses and the world;
When now the noise of many feet drew nigh
Softly approaching: and Seth spoke again,
"Behold! thy sons, thy messengers are here."
He drew the matted curtains of the tent
Aside, and Adam raised his head and saw
All his assembled children coming on,
Hushing their steps in awe; they stopped at gaze
Now as his eyes were on them; but before
Came the two messengers and stood alone.
How soiled and burnt with travel! Round the neck

Of Ophir hung the leopard's spotty hide
Stripped from that fierce beast strangled by his hand,
Torn now and stained; neither had paused to wash
The thick dust from his feet; but Iddo held
A spray of leaves new-plucked to freshen him
Seared on the parching mountain; thus they stood
With troubled countenance and hanging head
Till Ophir spoke; all listened rapt and still.
"Father, we went; and lo, we are come back
On the tenth morn, according to thy word.
For we have sought Cain but have found him not.
We passed beyond the mountains and we crossed
The sultry desert, toiling in hot sands
Two heavy days, and thence with difficulty
Climbed the far ridge unto the land beyond.
It is a land not fruitful like our vale,
Barren it is with short grass and few trees;
On the fifth day we came into the midst
Of that bare country and we saw no man,
Nor knew we whither to direct our steps,
When on a slope at unawares we spied
A sheepfold made of stones, and Lo! we said
To one another, Surely he was here.
Then eagerly we climbed the highest hill
And all around gazed long, but saw no more.
But toward the evening, when the light was low
And the extremest mountains grew distinct.
Far off in the clear air, but very far.
We saw a little smoke go up to heaven,
And we cried out. It is the home of Cain!
But deeply we were troubled and perplext.
For we were faint and footsore, and thy word
Lay heavy on our thoughts, remembering it,
On the tenth morning see that ye be here!
Surely our hearts were eager to go on;
But thinking of thy word we feared to go.
And hardly even now are we returned.
Father, we did thy bidding. Is it well?"
All gathered nearer, hushed and wistful; all
Awaited Adam's voice, but he was mute.
They would have prayed him, but they ventured not;
Like hunters that at hot noon, lost in woods,
Pressing through boughs and briers, at unawares
Come on the huge throat of a hollow cliff
Ribbed with impending ledges of wet moss,
Whence in a smooth-lipped basin of black stone
Some secret water wells without a sound:
Then sorely though they thirst they fear to drink,

Awed by the mystery of that silent source,
So these awhile with beating hearts delayed
To speak, awaiting what his words might be.
At last he raised his head and turned his eyes
On Eve, and looked upon her long, while she
On him hung gazing: light began to burn
In his dimmed eyes, and his whole frame was wrought
With the stirring of his spirit, as of old.
At length the thoughts were kindled on his tongue:
He lifted up his voice and cried aloud.

"O that mine eyes had seen thee once again,
Cain, that my hands had blessed thee! Thou art gone,
For ever gone, and still that curse abides
On thee who wast my joy, my first-born child.
Eve, Eve, hast thou forgotten that far hour.
When our first child, our baby newly-born.
Held up his little and defenceless hands
Crying toward thy bosom?" And Eve sighed:
"Surely my bosom hath not forgotten Cain,
Who sucked the tender first milk from its paps.
His feet are worn, wandering the desert wide,
But I have washed them with my tears in dreams.
O, in my heart he has not left his home.
Would I might lay my arms about him now!
Yet why, O Adam, utterest thou these thoughts?
Thou knowest how betwixt us and our son
There lies a land we may not overleap
More than the flames of those exiling swords,
Because of our fault, Adam, and of his.
Why dost thou waken this our ancient pain?"
But Adam still uplifted his lament:
"He is gone from us, gone beyond our reach,
Beyond our yearning, he remembers not
These arms that were around his weakness once.
These hands that fed him and that fostered him
And now would bless him. All these have I blessed
With many blessings, but him whom I cursed
Him would I bless at last, and be at peace.
He is gone from me, and now these also go
Whither I know not, and I fear for them.
How often have I seen them going forth
Into the woods upon these hills, how oft
See them with night returning, but now they
Depart for ever and return no more,"
Eve wondering replied with earnest voice,
"Behold them, Adam, they are very fair
And strong with all the strength that we have lost.

What ill shall harm them more than hath harmed us?
Remember how when I was used to fear,
Beholding our first child in his soft youth
Go from us on his tender feet alone —
His tender feet a little stone might bruise,
And would have caught him back to my fond breast,
Thou didst rebuke me, saying it must be
That he go forth alone; now thou dost fear,
When these are strong and we can help no more,"

But Adam shook his head and answered not.
For he was like a shepherd who hath lit
A fire to warm him on the mountain side.
In the first chill after the summer heats.
And drowsing by the embers wakes anon
With wonder-frighted eyes, to see the sparks
Blowing astray run kindling over grass
And withered heath and bushes of dry furze.
And ere his heavy senses, pricked with smoke,
Uncloud, the white fire rushes from his reach.
Leaps to embrace the tall pines, tossing up
A surge of trembling stars, and eagerly
Roars through their topmost branches, wide aflame,
While all around enormous shadows rock
And wrestle, as tumultuous light overrides
The darkness as with charging spears and plumes,
Till the whole hillside reddens, and beyond
Far mountains waken flushed out of the night:
Then he who ignorantly had started up
This wild exulting glory from its sleep
Forgets to stir his steps or wring his hands;
The swiftness and the radiance and the sound
Beget a kind of rapture in his dread;
Like that amazed shepherd Adam saw
His race, sprung out of darkness, fill the earth
Increasing swift and terrible like fire
That feeds on all it ruins, wave on wave
Streaming impetuous without rest or pause
Right onward to the boundaries of the world:
And he how helpless who had caused it all!
So stood his soul still in a gaze of awe
Filled with the foretaste of calamity:
And his lips broke into a groaning cry.
"What is this thing that I have done, what doom,
What boundless and irrevocable doom,
My children, have I wakened for you all?
O could I see the end, but end is none.
My thoughts are carried from me, and they faint.

As birds that come from out the farthest sky.
Voyaging to a home far, far beyond.
Sink in our valley on a drooping wing
Quite wearied out, yea, we have seen them sink.
So my thoughts faint within my bosom old;
The vision is too vast, I am afraid."

But understanding nothing of his speech,
That yet seemed opening some mysterious door
Disclosing an horizon all unknown,
His children listened, touched to trouble vague
And longing without name: like travellers
Who in a company together pass
On some spring evening by an upland road,
And as they travel, each in thought immersed,
Rich merchants, wise in profitable cares,
Adventurous youths, and timorous old men,
Through deepening twilight the young rising moon
Begins to cast along them a mild gleam.
And shadows trembling from the wayside trees
In early leaf steal forward on the ground
Beside them, and faint balm is past them blown;
All troubles them with beauty fresh and strange.
Stealing their thoughts away; so tenderly
Were Adam's children troubled when they heard.

Long silence fell. At last with heavy voice
And weakened utterance Adam spoke again:
"My children, bring me fruits and bring me flowers.
Set them within my sight that I may see
And touch them, and their sweetness smell once more."
They hasted and plucked flowers and gathered fruit
Such as their valley yielded; balsam boughs.
Late roses, darkly flushed, or honey-pale.
And heavy clustered grapes, and yellowing gourds,
Flump figs, and dew-moist apples, and smooth pears.
All these they brought and heaped before his sight
Voyagers in the utmost seas, when ice
Finions their vessel fast and they prepare
For the blind frozen winter's boundless night.
How jealously they watch the last low rays.
How from the loftiest vantage in their view
Cherish the rosy warmth still on their limbs,
Tarrying until the bright rim wholly dips!
Adam, by huger darkness overhung,
So longed to taste life warm even to the last;
And fostering those fair flowers upon his lap
And holding a gold apple in his hand

Remembered Eden. O what blissful light
Flowed o'er his heart and bathed it in its beams!
It seemed the deep recesses of his soul
Welled up their inmost wisdom at the last:
He glowed with some transfiguring fire; his lips
Moved, and his face uplifted was inscribed
With mighty thoughts, that thus at length unrolled
Their solemnly assembled syllables,

"Look well on me, my children, whom ye lose!
Behold these eyes that have wept tears for you.
Behold these arms that have long toiled for you! —
These hands in Paradise have gathered flowers;
These limbs, which ye have seen so wasted down
In feebleness, so utterly brought low,
They grew not into stature like your limbs,
I wailed not into this great world a child
Helpless and speechless, understanding naught.
But from God's rapture perfect and full-grown
I suddenly awoke out of the dark.
How sweet a languor did enrich the blood
In my warmed veins, as on my opening eyes
The splendour of the world shone slowly in,
Mingling its radiant colours in my soul!
Yea, in my soul and only in my soul
I deemed them to abide: sky, water, trees.
The moving shadows and the tender light.
This solid earth, this wide and teeming earth,
Which we have trodden, weary step by step,
Nor found beginning of an end of it,
I deemed it all abounding in my brain:
The murmur of the waters and the winds
Seemed but a music sighing from my joy;
Then I arose, and ventured forth afoot;
And soon, how soon, was dispossessed of all!
By every step I travelled into truth
That stripped me of my proud dreams, one by one,
Till all were taken. On such faltering feet
By gradual but most certain steps I came
Into my real and perfect solitude.
Alone amid the world that knew not me.
O Eve, thou knowest what I tell not now.
How I was comforted, and all the woe
That fell on our transgression; yet not less
When that first child lay babbling on thy knees.
Then again said I, 'Surely this is mine.'
And you, my children, whom I saw increase
Around me, stronger as my strength decayed.

How often have I called you also mine!
But now my first-born is not any more.
Or wanders lost from me, and ye, ye too
Go from me over earth, forgetting me.
So surely I perceive, for all that I
In joy begot you, ye are mine no more.
But ye, who seem the proud and easy lords
Of this fair earth, ye too must tread the path
Which I trod in my ignorant longing, lose
What I have lost, and find what I have found.
What seek you, O my children, what seek you?
For I behold you in this narrow vale.
That mountains and deep forests compass round
Filled with desires. Beyond is all the world
That hardly shall content them; ye must go
Forth into that vast world, as from my feet
This water glides, we know not whither; yea.
Even as this stream is prisoned in its speed,
So shall ye be imprisoned in desire.
But when you have imagined peace and balm
For your endeavour, musing, 'This is mine,'
When you shall say, 'I have a cause for joy,'
Then be distrustful, lest you only learn
How cruel is desire till it attain,
And being baffled yet more cruel grows.
Indignant not to find what it had sought.
And suffering ye rage, and raging fall
Upon your own flesh. Ah, deal tenderly
With one another, O my sons, for ye,
Caged in these limbs that toil under the noon,
Are capable of sorrow huge as night;
And still must ye bear all, whatever come.
Look how the trees in an untimely spring
Put forth their sweet shoots on the frosty air
That withers up the tender sap, yet still
Cannot delay their ripening, nor fold back
Their wounded buds into the sheltering rind;
So shall ye shrink, yet so must ye endure.
I that was strong and proud in strength, and now
Am come to this last weakness, tell you this:
Alas, could ye but know it as I know.
I speak in vain, ye cannot understand."

He ended sighing: for his mind was filled
With apprehensions rolling up from far
The doom and tribulation of his race.
Looking upon the faces of his sons.
Well he divined their weakness from his own.

He knew what they should suffer; yet the worst
He knew not; had he known, he would have rued
Less to be parent of their feebleness
Than of their strength, the power to maim and rend
And ravage even that which to their hearts
Is dearest, though they know not what they do,
Trampling their peace in dust; had he seen all
The dreadful actors on the endless stage.
Sprung from his loins, — ^the triumphing blind hordes,
Spurred by an ignorant fury to create
An engine of fierce pleasure in the pangs
Wrung from the brave, the gentle, and the wise.
And raging at a beauty not their own
That vexes all their vileness; till the world.
Discovering too late its precious loss.
Loves and laments in vain: had he seen this,
His grief had gone forth in a bitterer cry.
But they that heard him heard incredulous.
Trouble was far, and sweet youth in their hearts.
The beauty of the world encompassed them;
All else was fable; and they stood elate
Yet stirred and pensive, in such wondering pause
As might a troop of children who have found
In a king's garden, under shadowy yews.
Ancestral marbles on a sculptured wall.
Half hid in vines, and lifting up the leaves
Gaze in a bright-eyed wonder on fair shapes
Of arming heroes and unhappy queens.
Or press soft lips on Helen's woeful mouth,
Touching her perfect breast, and smile on her.
Unknowing how beneath that heavenly mould
Swelled, like a sea, the powers of love and pain,
Powers that shall surely also rock themselves
In storms, and their young courage crush to sobs.
Toss them on easeless beds, blind their hot eyes
With tears, in longing violent as vain,
Till they shall quite forget how life was once
Sweet as a rose's breath and only fair,
As now 'tis fair and sweet to Adam's sons.
Exalted in expectancy, they mused.
And in their veins a warmer current glowed
Round their full-moulded limbs; their open eyes
Shone wistful, and they murmured to themselves.
When Adam's voice recalled them to his grief
Out of unfathomable deeps his words
Seemed drawn in solemn slowness. "Lo, the light
Makes ready to go from you, even as I.
Hearken, my sons! Upon the mountain side

There is a cave that looks toward the East:
And thence in the evening clearness have I oft
Far-off beheld the gates of Paradise.
Mine eyes would feel that glory once again
Ere they be turned for ever to the night
Therefore go down and strew a bed for me,
Lay me upon that bed and bear me up.
It grows late and I may not tarry more."

But now at last the certainty of woe
Smote through them, and they feared exceedingly.
Scarce knowing yet what this command might mean.
They would have stayed, but Adam with raised hands
Moved them unto his bidding; they went down
And busied them, most sadly, o'er that toil
By the stream's shore, plaiting a bed of withes,
And some prepared rough poles, some gathered leaves.
Adam with Eve remained alone; the light
Slept warm upon the grass and on their feet.
And round about them in the spacious tent
Struck upward hovering glories, pale and clear.
He turned to her those eyes which never yet
Sought there a solace or heart's ease in vain,
And spoke, "O Eve!" but even there his voice
Stopt in the shadow of his coming thoughts,
And he could say no more; but she came near
To lay her hands on his cold hands, and looked
On his bowed face, and with a soft reproach
Answered him, "Adam, thou didst say but now
That all were going from thee o'er the earth
And thou shouldst be alone, and none be thine.
And no companion with thee any more.
Am I not with thee? Shall I go from thee?
Am I not thine? Am I not wholly thine?"
Then Adam lifted up his fallen brow
And gently laid his great arms round her neck;
He looked into her eyes, into her soul.
The face of Eve was falling toward his breast;
Her hair with his was mingled; now no more
They spoke, for they had come beyond all words.
They spoke not, stirred not, but together leaned,
Grand in the marble gesture of a grief
Becalmed for ever in the certitude
Of this last hour that over them stood still.
Thus had they stayed, nor moved, nor heeded aught;
But 'twixt them and the light a shadow fell:
And Adam lifted up his eyes, and saw
Seth standing there; he knew the hour was come.

For lo, about the doorway were the sons
Of Adam all assembled, with their wives
And children weeping; they had brought a bed
Of plaited osiers heaped with leaves; and now
Laying him on that litter, silently
They lifted up the poles. Eve weeping sank
Upon her knees: she kissed the dear last kiss;
She held his body in her tender arms
One aching moment, then relinquished him.
Thus they began, the young men and the old,
To bear him forth, unwillingly, with slow
Sad footsteps planted on the yielding sand,
While all the women wailed and wept aloud.
Beating their breasts; they felt and were afraid
Yet understood not; their despair was blind.
But Eve, who understood her perfect loss
Even to the utmost pang, wept now no more.
Her daughters sobbing round her, hid their heads:
She only, with dim eyes, stretched forth her hands.

But they that bore the litter passed beside
The bright stream's pebbly margin; and with them
The bearded men and boys, all overcome
With desolating thoughts and silent fears,
Followed: soon slowly they began to climb
Slopes scattered darkly o'er their bossy knolls
With shadowy cedars, where the jutting ribs
Of grey rock interposed; until at last
They came to the great cavern in the cliff.
And rested, gazing backward o'er the vale
Reposing in the golden solitude.
Then Adam said, "Lift me, that I may see."
With careful arms they lifted him: he gazed
Down on the valley stretched out at his feet.
Marked with the shining stream; he saw beyond
Ranges of endless hills, and very far
On the remote horizon high and clear
Shone marvellous the gates of Paradise.
There was his home, his lost home, there the paths
His feet had trod in bliss and tears, the streams,
The heavenly trees that had o'ershadowed him,
Removed all into radiance, clear and strange
As to a fisher on dark Caspian waves,
Far from the land, appears the glimmering snow
Of Caucasus, already bathed in dawn.
Like a suspended opal huge in heaven.
And wonder awes him to remember how
Long happy mornings of his youth he strayed

Over those same far valleys of his home,
Now melted and subdued to phantom shade
Beneath that lonely mount hung in the dawn:
So over darkened intervening vales
Tinged in the sweet fire of the light's farewell.
Shone Eden upon Adam. Then he sighed
A sigh not all of grief, "It is enough.
Leave me, my children, to my peace; go ye
And comfort Eve, go, prosper and be blest."
They each turned fearfully to each, but Seth
Bowed down his head and hushed them with his hand.
Silent with running tears they wept farewell,
And, often looking backward, on slow feet
Moved down the wide slope. Adam was alone.
At last his eyes were closing, yet he saw
Dimly the shapes of his departing sons,
Inheriting their endless fate; for them
The world lay free, and all things possible.
Perchance his dying gaze, so satisfied,
Was lightened, and he saw how vast a scope
Ennobled them of power to dare beyond
Their mortal frailty in immortal deeds,
Exceeding their brief days in excellence,
Not with the easy victory of gods
Triumphant, but in suffering more divine;
Since that which drives them to unnumbered woes.
Their burning deep unquenchable desire.
Shall be their glory, and shall forge at last
From fiery pangs their everlasting peace.

TO THE SUMMER NIGHT

A sultry perfume of voluptuous June
Enchants the air still breathing of warm day;
But now the impassioned Night draws over, soon
To fold me, in this high hollow, quite away
From oaken groves beneath and glimmering bay
And valley rock-bestrewn;
From all but shadowy leaves and scented ground
And this intense blue slowly deepening round,
From all but thoughts of beauty and delight
And thee that stealest as with hair unbound
O'er the hushed earth, and lips sighing, enamoured Night

Not the fair vestal of the Spring's cold sky.
But flushed from the ancestral East, thy home,

Drowsing the land, thou stirrest joy to a sigh.
Longing to passion and wild thoughts, that roam
As through those hungering Asian forests come
Panthers of ardent eye;
While over worlds wandering extravagant,
Like some divine and naked Corybant,
Thou movest; dark woods tremble and suspire;
And mortal spirits for life's full fountain pant,
As in content awakes the genius of desire.

Richer than jewelled Indian realm is thine,
stepper from the mountain-tops! for whom
On viewless branches of the heavenly vine
The white stars cluster faint or thickly bloom
Through the sapphire abyss of glowing gloom.
Press out a magic wine
For me — I thirst — from that intensest height.
Where even our keen thought, outsoaring sight.
Faints and despairs, ay, from some virgin star
Brim me a cup of that untreasured light
Lone in a world unreached, abounding, and afar!

Most far is now most dear. Blot out the near!
Lost is the earth beneath me, lost the day's
Removed ambition, all that fretful sphere
Drowned in the dark, and quenched its trivial praise.
I would behold beyond a mortal's gaze,
Behold even now, ev'n here.
The beauty strange, the ecstasy extreme.
Of what should this divine gloom best beseem.
The bosom of a Goddess, or her hair.
Invisible and fragrant — gliding dream.
Yet near as my heart beating, of such charm aware.

Why have we toiled so patiently to bend
This bow of arduous life? Unto what mark?
For what have set to our desire no end,
Steered to the utmost stormy sea our bark,
Piercing with eagle thought the frozen dark,
Been bold and gay to spend
Our warm blood, hazarded wild odds, and let
The bright world perish? What far prize to get?
What thing is this no speech could ever frame.
Nor hundred creeds ever imprison yet?
We breathe for it, and die, yet never named its name.

Star-trembling Night, Mother of songs unsung
And leaves unborn beneath the barren rind,

Who findest for forbidden hope a tongue,
Who treasurest most the treasure undivined
And flowers that banquet but the careless wind;
To whom all joy is young;
Prophetess of the fire that one day leaping
Shall burn the world's corruption, of the sleeping
Swords that shall strike down tyrants from their throne,
Mother of faith, our frail thought onward sweeping.
Breathe nearer, whisper close, spells of the dear unknown.

O of thy fated children number me!
Now while the alien day deep-sunken lies
And only the awakened soul may see.
Far from the lips that flatter or despise,
Foster my fond hope with thy certainties,
From time's subjection free,
That I may woo from some bare branch a flower,
Yea, from this world a beauty and a power
She gives not of herself; sustain me still
Through the harsh day, through every taming hour.
To find thy promise truth, thy secret grace fulfil.

THE SNOWS OF SPRING

O wailing gust, what hast thou brought with thee,
What sting of desolation? But an hour
And brave was every shy new-opened flower
Smiling in sun beneath a budding tree.
Now over black hills the skies stoop and lour;
Now on this lonely upland the shrill blast
Thrusts under brown dead crumpled leaves to find
Soft primroses that were unfolding fast;
Now the fair Spring cries through the shuddering wood
Lamenting for her darlings to the wind
That ravishes their youth with laughter rude.

The whole air darkens, sweeping up in storm.
What breath is this of what far power that slays?
What God in blank and towering cloud arrays
His muffled, else intolerable form?
What beautiful Medusa's frozen gaze?
Lo, out of gloom the first flakes ^floating pale.
Lost like a dreamer's thoughts! They shall lie deep
To-morrow on green shoot, on petal frail
And living branches borne down in despair
By the mere weight of that soft-nesting sleep,

Though all the earth look still and white and fair.

Fantasmal and extreme as some blind plain
Upon the far side of the moon, unknown
Deep Polar solitudes of ice enthrone
In the white night of mountain and moraine
The Power of that cold Sleep that dwells alone,
Absolute in remotest idleness.
Yet from his fancied lips the freezing breath
Wandering about the world's warm wilderness
Has drifted on the north wind even hither
These gently whispering syllables of death
Among the English flowers, our Spring to wither.

Not only the brief tender flowers, ah me!
Suffer such desolation, but we too
Who boast our godlike liberty to do
Whatever we will, and range all climes, ev'n we
Must still abide its coming and our rue.
It breathes in viewless winds and gently falls
Over our spirits, till desire grown sere.
Faith frozen into words, custom like walls
Of stone imprison us, and we acquiesce.
O more than raging elements to fear
Is snow-soft death that comes like a caress.

Life lives for ever: Death of her knows naught.
Our souls through radiant mystery are led.
Clothed in fresh raiment as the old is shed.
But Death the unchanging has no aim, no thought,
Deaf, blind, indifferent, feeds not yet is fed,
Moves not yet crushes, is not rent yet rends:
For as from icebergs killing airs are blown,
His cold sleep to our life-warm ardour sends
Frost wreathing round us delicate as rime,
Making most real what should be dream alone
To the free spirit, the gnawing tooth of time.

Who shall escape, since death and life inweave
Their threads so subtly? Yet may truth be wooed
In our own natures, shaken off the brood
Of thoughts not ours, beliefs our lips believe
But our hearts own not, — alien fortitude.
These are of death; and with his realm conspire
Faint souls that drowse in ignorance unjust.
That with the world corrupt their true desire.
And dully hate and stagnantly despise.
Already they begin to die, to rust;

But those that love are always young and wise.

O Love, my Love, the dear light of whose eyes
Shines on the world to show me all things new,
Falsehood the falser and the true more true,
And tenfold precious all my soul must prize.
Since from our life's core love so deeply grew,
O let us cleave fast to the heavenly powers
That brought us this, whose unseen spirit flows
Pure as the wind and sensitive as flowers.
They are with us! Let the storm-gathering night
Cover the bleak earth with these whirling snows,
Our hands are joined, our hearts are brimmed with light.

A VISION OF RESURRECTION

The Genius of an hour that fading day
Resigned to wide-haired Night's impending brow
Stole me apart, I knew not where nor how,
And from my sense ravished the world away.
Rose in my view a visionary ground,
A rugged plain, beneath uncoloured skies.
There slowly in the midst without a sound
Upheaved a motion as of birth. I gazed.
When lo! a head, with upcast empty eyes
And semblance of dead shoulders' majesties,
Whose fleshless arms a marble breast upraised.

But even as this emerged, nor yet was free,
Behold it ripen into bloom and form,
The shrunk limbs round and into colour warm,
The hair spring new as leaves upon a tree.
And curl like small flames round the forehead fair.
At last the eyelids open wide: it seems
A glorious-statured youth that wakens there.
Casting his eyes in wonder down, to feel
This body that with clear blood newly teems,
How perfect, yet still heavy as from dreams,
And over it the ancient beauty steal.

O lost in musing recollection sweet,
What summoning cry thine age-long slumber stirred?
In that profound grave has thy cold ear heard
From heaven the mailed Archangel call, whose feet
Stand planted in the stream of stars, and whose
Time-shattering trump hath pealed to the world's core?

Yet still doth thy averted head refuse
To lift its eyes up; still thy spread hands lean
On earth, while pensive thou surveyest o'er
This radiant shape that all thy sorrows bore,
Strong now as if no pain had ever been.

What thoughts begin to glide upon thy brain,
And part thy lips with sighs? Is it some fear
'Mid flattering heavenly airs approaching near
This strange unproven peace to entertain?
Musing, " O rebel flesh, in my hard need
How often didst thou fail me! I know well
How thou didst make me suffer toil and bleed.
At once my prison and my enemy.
Dear body, I fear thee yet: dark rages dwell
Within thee: how shalt thou in peace excel?
How learn to bear perfect felicity?"

Nay, rather that fond wonder in thy look
Is wonder to have lost the thoughts that maim.
The wounds of evilly-invented shame
And fear that each sweet impulse overtook.
Now thou art free, and all thy being whole,
Perceivest in that peril-haunted earth
The fair and primal gestures of thy soul.
And knowest how all thy full completion fed.
The urging hungers, the sun-sweetened mirth;
Yea, finding even in those furies worth,
Which lacking, hardly art thou perfected.

What trees are these whose dim young branches rise
Above thee? Springing waters freshen sweet
New tender green for thee to pace and greet
The growing of the dawn of Paradise.
Thou gazest round thee with a listening face,
Hearkening perhaps to some far-floating song
Unheard of men. Ah, go not ere thy grace,
O glorified, of me be throughly learned!
But as I prayed in supplication strong
The vision faded, and the world, whose wrong
Mocks holy beauty and our desire, returned.

QUEEN VENUS

Queen Venus on a day of cloud
Forsook heaven's argent palaces,

Beneath the roofing vapours bowed
And sought a promontory loud
Far in the utmost seas.

There to a caverned shore she made retreat,
Where granite shoulders of the mountain slant
Down to wet ledges that the waters beat,
Haunted of gull and diving cormorant.
Her garment was of green that deeply glowed;
One foot beneath its fluttering border showed.
As on a rocky solitary seat,
Sitting with both hands clasped about her knee,
She gazed unmoving over restless sea,
Heard not the wild birds scream and circling soar
Up the black cliffs and round their craggy tops,
But watched the full waves towering toward the shore,
Heaved up and ever falling in dumb roar.
And snowed into a thousand stormy drops.
Gardens of sultry Paphos, far away
Your doves among the strewn rose-petals play!
But doves nor roses please her heart to-day,
Who, child of ocean, comes to taste once more
The sting and splendour of the ocean spray.

Out of the cold mist curling,
The waters onward hurling,
As if a wizard driving
A myriad rebel spirits swept them thither,
Mounting, despairing, crying, and ever striving,
Swell toward her feet and in a moment wither.
O, idly in the wells of Venus' eyes
Those perishing proud glories fall and rise.
Like to a mirror where have come and gone
Faces of pain and passion, nor have left
Of all the abandoned story of their sighs
An image more than where a moonbeam shone,
She sees, she hearkens, but of thought bereft;
Her gaze holds neither pity, fear, nor wonder:
Yet in the exultation and the thunder
Of those waves moving as to music rolled.
Wherein their briefness is a tone half-told,
A spirit lives that doth her spirit claim;
Then she remembers how she also came
From deep-moved waters tossing and uptorn.
And 'mid such bitter idle foam was born
The serene charm that sets the world aflame.

Throned in an immortal throne.

Beauty holds her perfect place,
Without memory and alone,
Whether passionately known,
Or of all unknown her face.
But O, we mortals, that tormented see
Glimpses of our far felicity,
We that like wild waters hurled
Against the blind rocks of the world,
Ever vainly seek to climb
An hour beyond the clutch of time;
We whom fathomless desire
Lifts and fills with glorious fire,
Yet even in our triumph shakes
With trembling and in weakness breaks —
Sudden comes the gloom, and we expire;
Had we but strength to dwell in
The music of our dream,
Lifted from those gulfs we fell in
On the pure and rhythmic stream,
Then though we like shattered waves
Vanished in forgotten graves,
From that music and that motion
Power should flow to boundless ocean,
And from tumult far upborne
On the tide of rapt endeavour,
Merging all its pains forlorn
In its fulness, should be born
Beauty that should burn for ever!

THE BELFRY

Dark is the stair, and humid the old walls
Wherein it winds, on worn stones, up the tower.
Only by loophole chinks at intervals
Pierces the late glow of this August hour.

Two truant children climb the stairway dark.
With joined hands, half in glee and half in fear.
The boy mounts brisk, the girl hangs back to hark
If the gruff sexton their light footstep hear.

Dazzled at last they gain the belfry-room.
Barred rays through shutters hover across the floor
Dancing in dust; so fresh they come from gloom
That breathless they pause wondering at the door.

How hushed it is! What smell of timbers old
From cobwebbed beams! The warm light here and there
Edging a darkness, sleeps in pools of gold,
Or weaves fantastic shadows through the air.

How motionless the huge bell! Straight and stiff,
Ropes through the floor rise to the rafters dim.
The shadowy round of metal hangs, as if
No force could ever lift its gleamy rim.

A child's awe, a child's wonder, who shall trace
What dumb thoughts on its waxen softness write
In such a spell-brimmed, time-forgotten place.
Bright in that strangeness of approaching night?

As these two gaze, their fingers tighter press;
For suddenly the slow bell upward heaves
Its vast mouth, the cords quiver at the stress.
And ere the heart prepare, the ear receives

Full on its delicate sense the plangent stroke
Of violent, iron, reverberating sound.
As if the tower in all its stones awoke,
Deep echoes tremble, again in clangour drowned,

That starts without a whir of frighted wings
And holds these young hearts shaken, hushed, and thrilled.
Like frail reeds in a rushing stream, like strings
Of music, or like trees with tempest filled.

And rolls in wide waves out o'er the lone land.
Tone following tone toward the far-setting sun.
Till where in fields long-shadowed reapers stand
Bowed heads look up, and lo, the day is done.

At last it ebbs. Then silence on the last
Vibrating murmur builds its gradual weight;
Another silence from that silence past,
Charged with the will of only sleeping Fate,

Such as some venturous listener appals
In world-old forest, when, untouched by hand.
Utterly ripe, a great tree crashing falls
And not a sound succeeds. The children stand

Rapt in that silence with the life-lit eye
Of expectation, and awe-parted lips;
Yet in their breasts the heart is beating high,

Flushed are they, tingling to the finger-tips

With a dim sense of the world's meaning changed.
And Time dissolved, and a lost freedom found.
As if the soul had glimpse of regions ranged
Ere she was born into these senses bound.

They know not yet. But surely once again
Some touch of chance, a thought upon some face,
A sunned wall, a far voice, still midnight rain.
Shall strike them home into this hour and place.

And seized by memory in profounder spell.
So shall they listen with suspended breath
While, like that solemnly awakened bell.
Life deepens out to mystery more than Death;

And thrilling fear, like hope, to grandeur grown,
Losing the world, lets, ocean-vast, inroll
The power and glory of all that is unknown
Yet seeks in us the secret and the soul.

LOOK NOT TOO DEEP

Look not too deep in my heart,
My beloved; nay, lean not too near
From the shores of thy peace, lest thou start
From the midst of thy sweet thoughts to hear
The sound of waters of pain,
Blindly knocking and thronging,
The waters of heavy longing.
That deep in my heart has lain.

Sleeplessly circle the waves
Far under, and dumbly resound
In throats of the sea-filled caves.
Where daylight wholly is drowned.
Where frail fair shells are scattered
And broken in random foam,
With weeds that have found no home,
And drift-wood of ships long shattered.

But I would, my belov'd, that for thee.
Who bring'st me a sky all blue.
My spirit were stilled as a sea
That the fires of the noon warm through,

When the waves have forgotten their sighs
And from shore unto shore are at rest.
As my whole soul bathes and is blest
In the peace of thy beautiful eyes.

HAREBELL AND PANSY

O'er the round throat her little head
Its gay delight upbuoys:
A harebell in the breeze of June
Hath such melodious poise;
And chiming with her heart, my heart
Is only hers and joy's.

But my heart takes a deeper thrill,
Her cheek a rarer bloom,
When the sad mood comes rich as glow
Of pansies dipped in gloom.
By some far shore she wanders — where?
And her eyes fill — for whom?

GRIEF

Grief is like a child,
Led with relentless hand
By a strange nurse, whose face
Seems never to have smiled,
Whose onward gaze severe
Slackens not, nor her pace,
Nor that child's faltering fear
Stoops she to understand.

So strides the world, while grief
Unwilling is borne on.
With ever lingering mind,
Through the strange days, alone.
Oh, like a fluttering leaf
On the ways of the strong wind,
Or pebbles helpless thrown
By night on a wild strand,
Lost are the thoughts of grief,
That none can understand!

LAMENT

Fall now, my cold thoughts, frozen fall
My sad thoughts, over my heart,
To be the tender burial
Of sweetness and of smart.

Fall soft as the snow, when all men sleep,
On copse and on bank forlorn,
That tenderly buries, yet buries deep
Frail violets, freshly born.

SURSUM COR!

Lament no more, my heart, lament no more,
Though all these clouds have covered up the light,
And thou, so far from shore,
Art baffled in mid flight;
Still proudly as in joy through sorrow soar!
As the wild swan,
Voyaging over dark and rising seas.
Into the stormy air adventures on
With wide unfaltering wings, the way he bore
When blue the water laughed beneath the breeze
And morning round the radiant beaches shone.
So thou through all this pain
Endure, my heart, whither thy course was bound;
Though never may the longed-for goal be found,
Thy steadfast will maintain.
Thou must not fail, for nothing yet hath failed
Which was to thee most dear and most adored;
Still glorious is Love, thy only lord.
Truth still is true, and sweetness still is sweet:
The high stars have not changed, nor the sun paled.
Still warmly, O my heart, and bravely beat.
Remember not how lovely was delight,
How piteous is pain.
Keep, keep thy passionate flight.
Nor find thy voyage vain.
Yea, till thou break, my heart, all meaner quest disdain.

EUROPE, MDCCCCI

TO NAPOLEON

Soars still thy spirit, Child of Fire?
Dost hear the camps of Europe hum?
On eagle wings dost hover nigher
At the far rolling of the drum?
To see the harvest thou hast sown
Smilest thou now, Napoleon?

Long had the world in blinded mirth
Or suffering patience dreamed content,
When lo! like thunder over earth
Thy challenge pealed, the skies were rent:
Thy terrible youth rose up alone
Against the old world on its throne.

With shuddering then the peoples gazed,
And such a stupor bound them dumb
As those fierce Colchian ranks amazed
Who saw the youthful Jason come.
And challenging the War God's name
Step forth, his fiery yoke to tame.

He took those dread bulls by the horn,
Harnessed their fury to his will,
And in the furrow swiftly torn
The dragon's teeth abroad did spill:
When lo! behind his trampling heel
The furrow flowered into steel!

A spear, a plume, a warrior sprung —
Arm'd gods in wrath by hundreds; he
Faced all, and full amidst them flung
His magic helmet: instantly
Their swords upon themselves they drew,
And shouting each the other slew.

But no Medean spell was thine,
Napoleon, nor anointed charm;
Thy will was as a fate divine
To wavering men who watched thine arm
Drive on through Europe old thy plough.
The harvest ripens even now!

Time's purple flauntings, king and crown,
Old custom's tall and idle weeds,
Were tossed aside and trampled down,
While thou didst scatter fiery seeds,

That in the gendering lap of earth
Prepared a new world's Titan birth.

Then in thy path from underground,
Where long benumbed in trance they froze.
The Nations, giant forms unbound,
Slow to their aching stature rose;
And through their wintry veins again
Slow flushed the streams of life in pain.

Thy thunder, O Napoleon, passed,
But these whom thou hadst stirred to life.
On them the imperious doom was cast
Of inextinguishable strife.
For peace they longed, but blood and tears
Still blinded the tempestuous years.

A hundred years have flown, and still
For peace they pine; peace tarries yet.
These groaning armies Europe fill,
And war's red planet hath not set
O mockery of peace, that gnaws
Their hearts for so abhorred a cause!

Is peace so easy? Nay, the names
That are most dear and most divine
To men, are like the heavenly flames
That farthest from possession shine.
Peace, love, truth, freedom, unto these
The way is through the storming seas.

Ye wakened nations, now no more
You battle for a monarch's whim;
The cause is now in your heart's core,
Your soul must strive through every limb;
They who with all their soul contend
Bear more, but to a nobler end.

Be patient in your strife! And thou,
O England, dearer than the rest;
England, with proud looks on thy brow,
England, with trouble at thy breast,
Seek on in patient fortitude
Strong peace, most worthy to be wooed.

Take up thy task, O nobly born!
With both hands grasp thy destiny.
Easy is ignorance, easy scorn,

And fluent pride, unworthy thee.
Grand rolls the planet of thy fate:
Be thy just passions also great!

Turn from the sweet lure of content,
Rise up among the courts of ease;
Be all thy will as a bow bent.
Thy sure on-coming like thy seas.
Purge clear within thy deep desires
To be our burning altar-fires!

Then welcome peril, so it bring
Thy true soul leaping into light;
A glory for our mouths to sing
And for our deeds to match in might,
Till thou at last our hope enthrone.
And make indeed thy peace our own.

UMBRIA

Deep Italian day with a wide-washed splendour fills
Umbria green with valleys, blue with a hundred hills.
Dim in the south Soracte, a far rock faint as a cloud
Rumours Rome, that of old spoke over earth, "Thou art mine!"
Mountain shouldering mountain circles us forest-browed
Heaped upon each horizon in fair uneven line;
And white as on builded altars tipped with a vestal flame
City on city afar from the thrones of the mountains shine,
Kindling, for us that name them, many a memoried fame.
Out of the murmuring ages, flushing the heart like wine.
Pilgrim-desired Assisi is there; Spoleto proud
With Rome's imperial arches, with hanging woods divine:
Monte Falco hovers above the hazy vale
Of sweet Clitumnus loitering under poplars pale;
O'er Foligno, Trevi clings upon Apennine.
And over this Umbrian earth — from where with bright snow spread
Towers abrupt Leonessa, huge, like a dragon's chine,
To western Ammiata's mist-apparelled head,
Ammiata that sailors watch on wide Tyrrhenian waves, —
Lie in the jealous gloom of cold and secret shrine
Or Gorgon-sculptured chamber hewn in old rock caves,
Hiding their dreams from the light, the austere Etruscan dead.
O lone forests of oak and little cyclamens red
Flowering under shadowy silent boughs benign!
Streams that wander beneath us over a pebbly bed!
Hedges of dewy hawthorn and wild woodbine!

Now as the eastern ranges flush and the high air chills
Blurring meadowy vale, blackening heaths of pine.
Now as in distant Todi, loftily-towered — a sign
To wearying travellers — lights o'er hollow Tiber gleam,
Now our voices are stilled and our eyes are given to a dream,
As night, upbringing o'er us the ancient stars anew.
Stars that triumphing Caesar and tender Francis knew.
With fancied voices mild, august, immortal, fills
Umbria dim with valleys, dark with a hundred hills.

S. FRANCESCO DEL DESERTO

Peace in smooth summer hour
Paces the seas awhile;
But Peace has built her tower
Upon this chosen isle.

Scarcely a ripple stirs
In this lone shore's recess,
Scarcely a motion blurs
The mirrored cypresses

Ranked on a crumbling wall,
O'er slopes of flowery grass;
Where their long shadows fall,
Butterflies gleam and pass.

The idle sunshine sleeps
Before a porch; within,
Cool the white cloister keeps
Peace that has always been.

Beyond, a tangled plot
Of garden and tall trees.
Soothing its fragrance hot
In freshness from the seas.

There young monks slowly pace
With seldom-lifted eyes,
With world-unwritten face.
Not mournful yet nor wise.

Have they in this fair fold
Lost the fierce world in truth?
Or must the storms of old
Still shake the heart of youth?

Far in blue northern haze
The vast Alps glimmer pale,
Faint through the slumbrous blaze
Comes the white sea-gull's wail.

A DREAM

Behold an endless evening over land
That lapped in vast vales rises up afar
Into the frozen mountains; evening brimmed
With silence, so miraculously clear
That crevices in peaks of distant stone
And rust-red boughs of cedars, at the foot
Of those remote and voiceless waterfalls,
Which down the black steeps of lone gorges plunge,
Are shaped distinct unto the wondering eye;
And the mind, seeing, notes not how 'tis fair.
But throned in languor has already summ'd
All the vain journey thither. Not a sound
Near by; no motion lifts a single leaf.
Nor stirs one cold stalk of the sappy spurge
And powdery hemlock, nor 'mid clustered reeds
The peeping heads of certain dim blue flowers
Mirrored in water idle as themselves.
And she that sits upon the bank, whose head
Droops toward her shoulder, whose full lips are closed,
And whose wide eyes seem vacant, yet contain
Profound remembrance sunken like a wreck
Beneath gray seas, is she of this entranced
And glimmering land the sole inhabitant?

THE TUNNEL

Sitting with strangers in the hurrying train,
We spoke not to each other. Golden May
Flooded those warm fields greener from the rain,
Then sudden darkness stole it all away.

Her face was gone; but on the dark I framed
Its features, to my fancy's utmost height.
And with love's utmost fondness, never named,
Painted the image of my life's delight.

But lo! a gleam the window's edge outlined,
And beautifully dawning through the gloom.
She came back, O how much more than my mind
Had pictured, triumphing in breath and bloom!

Then I, ashamed, gave thanks with joy; I knew
That my best dream was bettered by the true.

AN HOUR

Together by bright water
We sat, my love and I.
Light as a skimming swallow
The perfect hour went by
With words like ripples breaking
On full thoughts softly waking;
With thoughts so dear and shy
That no word dared to follow.

Down by that sunny water
The spring's sweet voice we heard.
The wind, the leaves' young lover,
My love's hair gently stirred.
An hour ago we parted;
I wander heavy-hearted.
Heavily, like a wounded bird.
The day lags, night draws over.

AT EVENING

Fly home, my thoughts, that fretting
In alien words all day,
Have longed for the sun's setting
And wished all words away.
Fly home to her that knows you,
And in her heart repose you.

Fly home, my thoughts, and flutter
Like doves to gentle hands.
You need no lips to utter
What her heart well understands.
Her heart will open to you:
From far, my thoughts, she knew you.

Breathe out your breath, like roses.

About her loosened hair;
Soothe each eyelid that closes
With tender murmured prayer;
Your happy vigil keeping
Over her sacred sleeping.

Fly home, my thought's devotion,
Fly fast and there abide.
A barren senseless ocean
Is all the world beside.
Your home is only there, where she
Shrines all the world's desire for me.

A HYMN OF LOVE

Hush, sweet birds, that linger in lonely song!
Hold in your evening fragrance, wet May-bloom!
But drooping branches and leaves that greenly throng,
Darken and cover me over in tenderer gloom.
As a water-lily unclosing on some shy pool.
Filled with rain, upon tremulous water lying.
With joy afraid to speak, yet fain to be sighing
Its riches out, my heart is full, too full.

Votaries that have veiled their secret shrine
In veils of incense falteringly that rise.
And stealing in milky clouds of wavering line
Round soaring pillars hang like adoring sighs,
They watch the smoke ascending soft as thought,
Till wide in the fragrant dimness peace is shed,
And out of their perfect vision the world is fled.
Because the heart sees pure when the eye sees not.

I too will veil my joy that is too divine
For my heart to comprehend or tongue to speak.
The whole earth is my temple, and Love the shrine
That all the hearts of the world worship and seek.

But the incense cloud I burn to veil my bliss
Is woven of air and waters and living sun,
Colour and odour and music and light made one.
Come down, O night, and take from me all but this!

I dreamed of wonders strange in a strange air;
But this my joy, my dream, my wonder, is near
As grass to the earth, that clings so close and fair,

Nourished by all it nourishes. O most dear,
I dreamed of beauty pacing enchanted ground,
But you with beauty over my waiting soul.
As the blood steals over the cheek at a heart-throb, stole!
In the beating of my heart I have known you, I have found.

Incredulous world be far, and tongues profane!
For now in my spirit there burns a steadfast faith.
No longer I fear you, earth's sad bondage vain.
Nor prison walls of Time, nor the gates of Death.
For the marvel that was most marvellous is most true;
To the music that moves the universe moves my heart,
And the song of the starry worlds I sing apart
In the night and shadow and stillness. Love, for you.

BAHRAM THE HUNTER

When Bahrain rode to the chase,
Then saw ye his soul's delight
Full on his kingly face.
Who could his steed outpace?
He swooped like a falcon's flight;
Like a sunbeam that strikes from a cloud,
Exulting and eager-browed,
So rode he his reckless race.

Bright flashed the pools at morn,
And the sun o'er the mountains burned
And gilded the antelope's horn
In the plain, and the wild ass in scorn
Of the hunter the hard soil spurned.
Snuffing the wind, most fleet
Of quarries, the beat of whose feet
Is music to kings' ears borne.

Bahram smiled as he rode
On the dew-starred turf; debonair
Was his look, and his glad voice flowed.
White was the horse he bestrode,
And over his black beard and hair
The white-furred cap on his head
Was hung with tassels of red:
On his mantle a gold sun glowed.

And round him glittering gay
Rode princes and lords; he turned

To each with a word to say
In his royal courtesy; nay,
Not a heart but joyously burned
To be near to a heart so great,
And was fain to be proved its mate
In a glorious deed this day.

But the king's men shouted; for lo!
The wild ass afar they espied
In the shallowing valley below.
Where bright springs fathomless flow.
He was shaking his neck in pride,
And his heels the dust upthrew:
Then Bahram shot forth to pursue.
As a bolt that is shot from a bow.

The princes of Persia spurred,
But he left them all; this day
There was neither second nor third
To the king. Now a startled bird
From the low grove fluttered away;
Then the plain smoked up in a cloud
Behind them, and thundered aloud;
Yet never the king they neared.

Swifter the onaga fled,
But swifter the king came nigher,
Wherever those fleet heels led;
Now soft upon grass he sped,
Now the hoofs upon stone struck fire;
Till the wild ass turned in his fear
For an instant, and showed him clear
The eyeball strained in his head.

Then the princes shouted as one.
For they heard the king's glad shout.
And saw his spear raised in the sun,
And the light o'er the long shaft run;
As they looked for the steel to flash out
On a sudden the place was bare;
Bahram was no more there,
And the onaga galloped alone.

Pale they spurred o'er the ground
Then reined in close with a cry.
Gazing in terror around:
Neither king nor horse they found.
But before them laughed to the sky

A pool of springs that well
From the streams under earth and swell
Through her secret caverns profound.

The women of Shiraz wail,
And the young men cry in the street,
"No more now in the Vale
Of Heroes shall Bahram hail
His quarry of glancing feet,
No more shall his voice delight
Our hearts through the battle, and smite
The ranks of the Tartar pale!"

The mother of Bahram hath made
Amid pillars his empty tomb
Of porphyry, jasper, and jade.
Clear gums in fire she hath frayed
To cloud it in idle fume.
Yet riches from isles of the dawn.
Nor spices from far Damaun,
Lure hither the strong-winged shade.

Tomb nor prison shall tame
Bahram the hunter's soul.
As of old to the chase he came.
He is turned not aside from his aim.
He is mixed with the streams that roll
Unending as man's desire,
That shall not abate of its fire
Till the whole world crumble in flame.

THE DESERTED PALACE

"My feet are dead, the cold rain beats my face!"
"Courage, sweet love, this tempest is our friend!"
"Yet O, shall we not rest a little space?
This city sleeps; some corner may defend
Our weary bodies till the storm amend."
"So tired, dear heart? Then we will seek some place
Safe from rude weather and this night air chill.
And prying eyes of those that mean us ill."

These lovers, fleeing through the midnight street.
Breathlessly pause amid the gusty moan
Of winds that have not heard their echoing feet
Blind houses, towering up, leave light alone

From narrow skies in glimmering swiftness blown:
In front, from vales of darkness wild airs beat;
Behind them, shouldering crests of cloudy pine
Looms, lost in heaven, the cloven Apennine.

Down the strange street their doubtful steps explore
Each shadowy archway, angle, and recess,
For shelter, nor have travelled far before
Giselda, half-despaired for weariness,
Feels on her fingers Raymond lightly press;
Heavy above the surging wind's uproar
With a dull echo, clanging now, then drowned,
Reverberates a sullen stormy sound.

What heart so fixed that darkness cannot shock?
When the mind stumbles with the blind footfall,
What world may not a random sound unlock,
Wild as a fever-dream's original.
Where through black void we should for ever fall.
Did not our hearts freeze as in dungeon rock?
So Night may mask, when reason, numbed in trance.
Quails at the wandering cyclops, idiot Chance.

Beyond a buttress both had crept more near.
In this dim wall was it a gate that swung?
Still hesitating, half-bewitched in fear.
Upon the silent intervals they hung.
Again it clanged as if the senseless tongue
Of Chaos knelled upon the startled ear.
Resounding mockery of that tranquil, bright
Well-featured earth men fable in daylight.

A gate so old it leaned and swung awry,
With such indifferent motion to and fro
As a stone rolled by shore waves fitfully,
Heavy and melancholy, wavering slow,
Then closed and clashing with a sudden blow:
To what forlorn abode, left long to lie
For spider, gray owl, and the blind bat's wing,
Could this be door? What ruin mouldering?

Raymond with doubtful hand felt on the bar
Rusty and wet; pushed slow the ponderous wood
That gaped on blackness; moaning from afar
A riotous gust rolled back the hinge; he stood,
And leaning pressed the dark weight all he could;
Again it yielded with a grinding jar;
They entered, where they knew not; empty ground

Seemed closed by heights of doubled gloom around.

"What place is this? My feet tread soft on grass,"
Giselda whispered. Raymond drew her on.
Across what seemed a weed-grown court they pass —
Black walls around them, heaven above them wan —
Till soon a row of pillars dimly shone
Before them, o'er wet marble steps. "Alas!
I fear," she cried; but he drew close to his
Her cheek, and made her blood brave with a kiss.

Wondering in that deserted colonnade,
They hearkened to the storm, less boisterous there.
Till to their peering sight a hollower shade
Signalled a doorway deep in quiet air;
And now their hearts beat at an omen fair;
For venturing hands, on either doorpost laid,
Found, sculptured there, soft features of a child,
Where, ignorant of darkness, beauty smiled.

As sailors, nearing home, but blown from land.
When the wind bears them scent of fields they knew;
As a blind father, when his son's young hand,
Laid confident on his, brings faith anew
In the lost light and the pure heavenly blue;
As homeless Psyche, when she trembling scanned
Love's fair strange house, and a mild voice drew near
Invisibly, and soothed away her fear.

So thrilled by silent sweet encouragement,
As if some guardian presence ministered
To aid them, onward, hand in hand, they went.
No living sound in all the place they heard;
Still on they groped, but not a form appeared;
Sometimes beneath an arch their heads were bent:
At last a window, pallid through the gloom,
Showed them each other 'mid an empty room.

Each in the other's face, with breathing stilled,
The tender bright eyes tenderly discerned;
And they embraced, while both their bosoms filled
With growing charm of peace so strangely earned.
Rapt thus they stood, nor any longer turned
At sudden gusts that through the midnight thrilled.
He smoothed the rain-drops from her hair that strayed;
She smiled and spoke: " I am no more afraid."

But soon a nest secure from wind they found,

Pillowing their cloaks against the corner wall,
And rested happy; there the roar was drowned,
And only in subsiding interval
Of shuddering flaws, they heard the rushing fall
From rain-swept eaves; 'mid desolation round
Their hearts beat closer to each other, warm
Because of those wild blasts of wandering storm.

Giselda drooped her heavy-lidded eyes;
Tired out, her peaceful bosom sank and swelled:
Soft upon Raymond's shoulder breathed her sighs;
His fostering arm her leaning breast upheld;
Her drowsing head by slumber sweetly quelled
Now and then, lifted in a child's surprise.
Murmured, and soon from all the long day's ache
Slipped into sleep; but Raymond stayed awake.

Bold was his heart; yet extreme tenderness
For that dear heaven enfolded in his arm
Sharpened his fond thoughts to a strange distress.
Threatening his secret storm-encircled charm,
As by the violent waters walled from harm
Amidst the whirlpool's roaring heedlessness
A stillness keeps, most perfect, yet so frail,
That in an instant shattered it may fail.

Then he bethought him of what laughter dead
Had under those old rafters leapt and rung;
What companies of joy had banqueted;
What lovers listened and what ladies sung:
Here had they dwelt, been beautiful, been young!
He bent in tears above that precious head
Slumbering, a thousand times more dear than life,
By him, and whispered, " O my wife, my wife!

"Alas! what eager hearts and hands once wrought
This chosen place to fashion and adorn!
And now their names are faded out of thought,
And their fond toil neglected and forlorn.
This is their grave. O would that it were morn!
All my great love in this dark house seems naught.
And I in a dead midnight-world alone.
Save for thy dear heart beating on my own.

"Beat close, warm heart, ere my sad spirit cower.
From those dead bosoms not a single sigh!
Year heaped on year, hour creeping over hour,
The wilderness of silence spreads more nigh.

And what a momentary moth am I!
Beat nearer, heart! tell me I still have power
To breathe, to move; I grow so faint and dead.
So Time's wide seas weigh heavy on my head!"

Thus murmuring with daunted forehead low
Leant to her breaths, he listened to the rain.
The gloom seemed living, seemed to tower and grow
O'er him, a shadow among shadows vain.
At last the thoughts grew cloudy in his brain;
The young blood in his wearied limbs grew slow;
His arms relaxed, and in his senses lulled
The sadness faded, exquisitely dulled.

Birds that have nested in tall elm-tree tops
Sleep not more sound, when winds that rock them roar,
Whirling dry leaves about the wintry copse.
Than both slept now, while on the wild night wore.
At last the storm ebbed and was heard no more,
Save in brief gusts and sudden shaken drops:
The dawn came hushed, and found each peaceful face
Turned to the other in entranced embrace.

Raymond awoke. It was the early light
That stole through half-closed shutters o'er the room:
With gleaming stillness it caressed his sight.
And on the floor lay tender like a bloom.
It seemed his own heart wholly to illume,
Soft as a smile, and growing slowly bright.
Spilled its reflected clearness everywhere
Into all corners of that chamber bare.

Slow in delicious languor turn his eyes
Wondering around him. Still Giselda dreams;
But all things else how new a wonder dyes!
From the sunned floor the young light upward gleams,
Hovers about the ceiling's coffered beams.
And those deep squares of shadow glorifies.
Smiling fresh colours on the cornice old
And shielded corbels' rich abraded gold;

Where underneath, in clear or faded stain.
The walls were pictured with old stories fair:
The selfsame walls that, prisoning his pain.
Gloomed yesternight so desolately bare
Now blushed and gloried in the morning air,
More beautiful in Time's enchanting wane,
As leaves by spoiling Autumn fostered few

Treasure the wonder of her tenderest hue.

On the left hand there was a wild seashore,
And Hero, leaning from her turret lone,
Gazed out impassioned where the surge upbore
Leander's face turned fainting to her own.
Careless of chill spray through her deep hair blown,
She stretched her arms, never to clasp him more.
Even now his hands were tossed up in the foam.
But from his eyes his soul leapt towards its home.

Upon the right flushed Cephalus hallooed,
Parting green thickets; knew his spear had sped,
But knew not yet the white doe of that wood
Was his own Procris. Low her piteous head
Lay on the grass; her bosom brightly bled,
And her lips trembling strove, while yet they could,
To pardon the dear hand that wrought that wound,
While dumbly she caressed his whimpering hound.

These upon either end wall were pourtrayed;
But in the midst was Orpheus with his lyre,
Singing to the ear of one beloved shade.
Lost somewhere in those aisles of gloomy fire.
Only for her he poured his soul's desire:
Yet the grim Pluto hearkened as he played,
And Proserpine remembered the sweet spring.
And with wet cheek besought him still to sing.

Eurydice, through darkness music-drawn,
Was gliding (none forbad her) toward his feet;
And other ghosts like, in the earliest dawn.
Sparrows that stir and raise their restless tweet,
Stole fluttering, because of sound so sweet,
Over the pale flowers of their shadowy lawn,
Lifting their drooping heads as they drew nigh;
And all those faces listening seemed to sigh.

Love, whom no goal, no haven satisfies.
Love hungered and athirst, bound, scarred, and lame.
Proud rebel, who through fading mortal eyes
Shoots beams of that clear fire Time cannot tame.
Burned here in suffering flesh his beacon flame.
Ah, who can read these passionate histories.
Nor feel vibrations as of music roll
Ennobling challenge to his kindled soul?

Raymond beheld them; and it seemed all time.

Till now a cave of dimness, without hue.
Flushed back love's colours from its farthest prime.
Claiming the sacrificial fire anew
From his full heart. Nay, every age foreknew
This moment, and the dumb years seemed to climb
Patiently growing toward this latest hour
That bore his own love like a folded flower.

He hung above her slumber, and he spelled
Upon her face the still soul unaware.
A whiter throat than Hero's sorrow swelled
Shone faint beside the flame-brown wave of hair:
But on her cheek the blood's clear tinge how rare!
And the red mouth, how sweet a song it held
Asleep until the living dawn should rise
Brimmed in the perfect sunbirth of her eyes!

O surely here the dead world's shadow-brood
Of spirits yearning from the misty tomb
Hung o'er the presage of earth's coming good,
And poured for her their prayerful hope, in whom
Life triumphing wore all their ravished bloom —
Soft image of immortal womanhood,
For whose dear sake the world waits in its need,
And heroes of the farthest age must bleed.

Raymond gazed on, and could not gaze his fill.
Rapt on a silent stream of thought afloat
The soft light stirred not; all the house was still;
Only at times with negligent sweet note
A thrush without would fill his freshened throat.
Where the sun slept on the warm window sill.
And in translucent leaves of trailing vine
Melted his glittering rays to golden wine.

Giselda's face gleamed in the shadowed light
He bent to wake her; then again delayed,
Lingering upon the foretaste of delight
"O you dear spirits," suddenly he prayed,
"Whose hearts imagined and whose hands arrayed
This home in beauty, ere you turned to night,
And having shed your grosser mortal part
Live in the beatings of the gazer's heart!

Peace be upon you, peace for ever be!
Let my lips bless you, whose bright faith unmarred
Shows me the core of my felicity.
And who, though deep in drear oblivion barred.

Committing Sorrow into Beauty's guard,
Pour your immortal ardour into me:
To such a faith all my desire I vow.
May it burn ever as 'tis kindled now!

Wake, love, awake. O thou art grown so dear.
Yet in the enriching beams of this new day
So glorious a spirit, I almost fear
That from sleep's prison thou wilt soar away
Beyond the stretching of my arms. Nay, nay,
I'll hazard hope for truth. Love, I am here.
Shine out thine answer from those opening eyes.
And lift my soul up into Paradise!"

Enraptured thus, he kissed her. She awoke.
Her gaze that wandered, anchored upon his
In happiness, and dreamingly she spoke:
"Do I sleep still? Or what fair house is this?
Smiling, he answered with joy's perfect kiss,
And raised her up and wrapt her in her cloak.
So both stole forth. The still world seemed to lie
Their radiant kingdom under the wide sky:
Young was the morning, and their hearts were high.

SANTA CRISTINA

At Tiro, in her father's tower,
The young Cristina had her bower.
Over blue Bolsena's lake.
Where small frolic ripples break
Under a grove of sycamore
On the sandy eastern shore.
There one clear May eve she sat
Leaning over the rich mat
Hung across the window-sill,
While her doves with eager bill
Fluttered round her for the grain
In her spread hands; up again
Now they soared through golden light,
Radiant in a swerve of white,
Round the trees, now scattering
With a shiver of many a wing.
Soft as snowy drops of foam
Singly they alighted home,
And swaying each a sheeny throat
Crooned their comfortable note.

On a sudden another sound
Smote Cristina from the ground,
Bending over, she espied
Wretched ragged folk, who cried,
Hoarsely: "See, the doves are fed;
We, men and women, have not bread."
While Cristina, with a shy.
Courteous simplicity,
Looked upon them, her young heart.
New to sorrow, felt the dart
Of pity pierce her body through.
And she spoke: "What must I do?"
Then with a thought her bosom beat.
And swift away on frightened feet
To her father's chapel, rich
With images in carven niche.
Breathless and bright-eyed she sped,
Most in dread of her own dread,
Traitor to her purpose; took
The idols in her hands that shook
And brought them gathered in her gown
And from the window cast them down.
The ragged people cried and snatched
This broken treasure; then were matched
Strange companions: here the bust
Of gazing Jupiter august
Weighed on a sore-blotched cripple; there
Against a scullion's clouted hair
Apollo's silver shoulder shone.
While, near by, a withered crone
Hugged into her bosom old
Venus' arm and breast of gold.
Mumbling o'er their spoils they went,
A troop to stir the merriment
Of gods; but sad Cristina sobbed.

When the stately father robbed,
Entering found his pagan shrine
Emptied of its works divine,
Each by a famous craftsman wrought,
Chosen well and dearly bought,
And suffered only to be scanned
(With fond touches of the hand)
By the nice appraising eye,
Duke Urban cried a grievous cry:
But when at last he understood
The crime of his own flesh and blood,

Grief was swallowed up in rage.
"Pest on this corrupted age!"
He cried. "This is this new god's work.
And now I find the venom lurk
In my own child, in my own home!
I am a citizen of Rome.
She shall have justice: take her hence,
And let my dungeon teach her sense."
Cristina weeping pleads the pain
Of the famished folk; in vain!
Straightway she is cast and bound
In a dungeon underground.
Three days went "Now bring her out,"
Said Urban. Servants, much in doubt,
Led her from the dungeon door,
Much in doubt yet wondering more.
For the damp and starving gloom
Had but glorified her bloom.
And her brow was brave, as she
Stepped before her father: he
With a sullen doubtful glance
Some moments looked on her askance.
"Art thou taught?" at last he said.
Proud she lifted up her head.
"Father, if I wronged thee, thou
Didst mar the face of mercy. Now,
By God's grace, thy cruel wrong
Hath but made my soul more strong.
I have suffered for thy pride:
Let thy poor be satisfied.
See, God stands upon my side!"
Duke Urban flushed an angry hue.
"Wilt thou brave me to thy rue.
Child?" he cried. "Since in thee still
Some imp of evil works his will.
Pricking thee outrageously,
I will burn him out of thee.
Go, build a furnace; bind her in.
And let the flame purge out her sin."
All her women wept, implored,
"Ah, be merciful, dear lord!"
But the more imperious came
His answer: "Cast her to the flame."

When that evening fell, a light
Rose and shuddered up the night.
On the reddened shore around
Soldiers kept the fiery ground,

Where amid the furnace stood
Cristina: spite of hardihood.
None but turned away his eye
To see so sweet a creature die.
Swifter roared the bright fire, dancing
Madder, on their armour glancing.
While the people kneeling wailed.
Suddenly all faces paled.
In their ears a clear voice sang.
From amidst the fire it sprang
Joyous; and the soldiers raised
Their heads, and all the people gazed;
There in the moving crimson core
Of the flames that sound and soar,
Coil and quiver, twist and spire,
'Mid the insuflerable fire.
Like a breathing beauteous rose.
Nay, like a precious vase that glows
Outlined intense and clear and white,
Absorbing all the burning light
Into its tissue, through and through.
To purify the shell-like hue.
They behold Cristina stand,
Lifting either little hand,
And with parted lips, and eyes
That the fierce flame glorifies,
See her form transfigured shine
Singing in that fiery shrine —
An embodied rapture! Awe
Fell upon all them that saw.
The young voice melted in their ears.
And beauty hushed them into tears.
Heaven seemed opening on their sight
To its inmost soul of light,
And the daily world of woes
Fell from off them, and they rose
In a rapture: faces, turned
Each unto his neighbour, burned.
While they cried with voices full,
"A miracle, a miracle!"

Urban in his dark tower heard
Trembling that exultant word.
Rage by stabbing terror spurred
Swelled his heart to madness. Straight
With a torch from the open gate
Striding he commanded: "Curst
Be this snake that I have nursed!

She has witched to her desire
A demon lover, a fiend of fire;
Yet she shall not 'scape me now.
Ere another night, I vow,
She shall die. With morning take
And throw her deep into the lake."

Though men groaned and women shrieked
At such cruel vengeance wreaked,
None this old man's rage gainsaid;
For within their hearts they prayed
Some new marvel should confound
All his fury.
Morning found,
On the glimmering shore assembled,
A great multitude that trembled
Half with hope and half with fear.
Hemmed behind the levelled spear
Of armed ranks; and over all,
Ringed by silent lances tall,
In a high seat Urban sat.
By threatening fingers pointed at,
Motionless with eager frown
And on the wide lake gazing down.
Soon the sun's uprising glowed
Over the eastern hill, and showed,
'Mid the waters that anew
Shivered silvering into blue,
A single boat; it brightly shone
Where Cristina knelt thereon,
And the hangman at her side
Busy bending over tied
Round her neck a great mill-stone;
In the water she was thrown.
Passionate arose the groan
From those watchers, but as soon
Changed into a paean's tune;
For she sank not, but was seen,
Where death's bubble should have been,
Standing on the stone that bore
Her bare feet floating toward the shore.
With little tremblings at the knees
As the buoyant, urging breeze
Rocked her onward. With a shout
Thronged the people, stretching out
Eager arms, or under spears
Thrust their heads with joyful tears.
Clapped their hands and cried to see

So magical a wonder. She,
Simple in her loveliness.
By one hand holding up her dress
From the wave that washed its hem
With white sparkle, seemed to them
Fresh as Venus on her shell
Borne o'er the blue Ionian swell.
Round her head the soft-blown hair
Played in sunny streams of air,
Save one long tress on her breast
That her clasping fingers pressed.
In a dream she heard the cries.
Saw the bright and crowding eyes
Near and nearer; when a strong
Sudden tumult rose; the throng
Turned, and lo! on his high chair,
'Mid the spearmen struggling there,
Duke Urban with head fallen back
And the full vein swollen black
On his throat: his fingers tear
At the suffocating fear
That holds him by the panting heart
Breathless, and his fixed eyes start,
While the heaving hubbub round
Rocks about him; in hoarse sound
Of vengeance his death-gasp is drowned.

But Cristina floating nigh
When she saw this, piteously
Bowed her gentle forehead low
In her hands, and cried, "Ah, woe
On me and mine! O Lord of Peace,
Now my wretchedness release!"
Even as in despair she prayed.
One that on the shore delayed
At the crowd's edge, watching all
And doubtful what might yet befall,
Scowled and said within his teeth,
"This witch-girl comes to be our death,"
Strung his bow and spurred by fear
Drew an arrow to his ear.
And while still this fierce uproar
Held the wild throng on the shore
Sharp upon the tender throat
The iron barb Cristina smote.
Ere a man had turned to note,
She was falling; ere a tongue
Had one cry of warning rung,

She had fallen, and the foam
Tossing shoreward washed her home.
As a sudden silence rushed
Over lips in terror hushed.
Rolled amid the shallow spray
At their feet her body lay.

Dark is the world to the weak will
As to feet stumbling on a hill
Benighted, when no stars appear.
But as a star that beacons clear,
O beauty of courage, thou dost shine
On souls that falter and that pine.
But most in bodies frail and young
Is thy beauty seen and sung.
There, like a fountain ever new,
Thou dost scatter sunny dew,
Troubling our self-bewildered night
With simplicity of light.
Therefore is Bolsena's lake
Dear for fair Cristina's sake.
Yea, the stone that bore her feet
And still bears the footprint sweet.
Housed in alabaster shrine
Of carved work, as a thing divine,
And by dead lips' kisses worn,
Shall be kissed in sorrow's scorn
By lips of thousands yet unborn.

WORDS

Words, breathing words, full-murmuring syllables!
How you enrich the thoughts that dwell in you
With far-brought perfume, that no meaning tells
Yet stirs the mind to flower in thoughts anew!

Sometimes how lulling like the rain's soft veil.
Then vivid as the pressure of a hand,
Now filled with fair surmises like a sail
Before the blue coast of some foreign land.

O words, you live and therefore you can die,
Ill-yoked, imprisoned, tamed in a dull task!
So callous tongues may use you, but not I,
Who for your grace, a wooing lover, ask.

Dead things may kill; and you being dead entomb
The frozen thought that once you clothed in bloom.

A PRAYER TO TIME

Move onward, Time, and bring us sooner free
From this self-clouding turmoil where we ply
On others' errands driven continually:
O lead us to our own souls, ere we die!

We toil for that we love not; thou concealest
Our true loves from us; all we thirst to attain
Thou darkly holdest, and alone revealest
A mirror that our sighs for ever stain.

Art thou so jealous of our full delight?
Thou takest our strength, toil, fervour, and sweet youth;
And when thou hast taken these, thou givest sight
At last to see and to endure the truth.

Thou art too swift to our weak steps; but oh.
To our desire thou movest. Time, how slow!

Laurence Binyon – A Short Biography

Robert Laurence Binyon, CH, was born on August 10th, 1869 in Lancaster in Lancashire, England to Quaker parents, Frederick Binyon and Mary Dockray.

He studied at St Paul's School, London before enrolling at Trinity College, Oxford, to read classics.

Binyon's first published work was Persephone in 1890. Whilst only a few pages in length it certainly illustrated the talents that Binyon would develop as a poet even though he continued to advance multiple career opportunities.

Immediately after graduating in 1893, Binyon started work at the British Museum for the Department of Printed Books, writing catalogues for the museum and art monographs for himself. As well as being one of England's best poets he was also renowned for his knowledge of various arts particularly with regard to Japan and Persia.

His first poetry book Lyric Poems was published in 1894.

In 1895 his first art book, Dutch Etchers of the Seventeenth Century, was published and, that same year, Binyon moved into the Museum's Department of Prints and Drawings.

Whilst Binyon became known to a wide audience as a poet his output was not prodigious. In 1898, Porphyrion & Other Poems was published followed by Odes (1901) and The Death of Adam & Other Poems (1904).

That same year, 1904, Binyon married the historian Cicely Margaret Powell. The union was to produce three daughters.

In the early years of the 20th Century Binyon was a regular patron of the Wiener Cafe of London together with fellow artists and intellectuals; Ezra Pound, Sir William Rothenstein, Walter Sickert, Charles Ricketts, Lucien Pissarro and Edmund Dulac.

His poetic work continued despite the demands of the British Museum and his other interests. London Visions was published in 1908 followed by England & Other Poems in 1909.

His work at the British Museum ensured promotions were a frequent occurrence for Binyon. In 1909, he became its Assistant Keeper, and in 1913 he was made the Keeper of the new Sub-Department of Oriental Prints and Drawings.

It was also at this time that he played a crucial role in the formation of Modernism in London by introducing young Imagist poets such as Ezra Pound, Richard Aldington and H.D. (Hilda Doolittle) to East Asian visual art and literature.

Many of Binyon's books produced while at the Museum were influenced by his own sensibilities as a poet, although some are clearly works of plain scholarship, such as his four volume catalogue of all the Museum's English drawings, and his seminal catalogue of Chinese and Japanese prints.

Binyon's poetic reputation before the war, although built on several slim volumes, was such that, on the death of the Poet Laureate Alfred Austin in 1913, Binyon was among the names considered as his likely successor. It was quite a field. Among the other illustrious contenders were Thomas Hardy, John Masefield and Rudyard Kipling; however the post was awarded to Robert Bridges.

Moved and shaken by the onset of the World War I and its military tactics of young men slaughtered to hold or gain a few yards of shell-shocked mud as the British Expeditionary Force began its campaign Binyon wrote his seminal poem For the Fallen, with its Ode of Remembrance (the third and fourth or simply the fourth stanza of the poem). The poem was published by The Times newspaper on September 21st, when public feeling was shaken by the recent Battle of Marne. It became an instant classic, turning moments of great loss into a National and human tribute.

Today, For the Fallen, is often recited at Remembrance Sunday services as well as being an integral part of Anzac Day services in Australia and New Zealand and of November 11th Remembrance Day services in Canada. The "Ode of Remembrance" is now acknowledged as a tribute to all casualties of war, irrespective of nation.

In 1915, despite being too old to enlist, Binyon volunteered at a British hospital for French soldiers, the Hôpital Temporaire d'Arc-en-Barrois, Haute-Marne, France, working for a short time as a hospital orderly.

He returned there in the summer of 1916 and took care of soldiers taken in from the Verdun battlefield. He wrote about his experiences in For Dauntless France (1918) and his poems, "Fetching the Wounded" and "The Distant Guns", were inspired by his hospital service.

After the war, he returned to the British Museum and wrote numerous books on art; especially on William Blake, Persian and Japanese art. His work on ancient Japanese and Chinese cultures offered inspiration that inspired many, among them the poets Ezra Pound and W. B. Yeats. His work on Blake and his followers kept alive the then nearly-forgotten memory of the work of Samuel Palmer. Binyon's spectrum of interests continued the traditional interest of British visionary Romanticism in the rich strangeness of Mediterranean and Oriental cultures.

In 1931, his two volume Collected Poems appeared and by 1932, Binyon was promoted to the post of Keeper of the Prints and Drawings Department. The following year, 1933, he retired from the British Museum. He went to live in the country at Westridge Green, near Streatley but continued writing poetry.

In 1933–1934, Binyon was appointed Norton Professor of Poetry at Harvard University. He delivered a series of lectures on The Spirit of Man in Asian Art, which were published in 1935.

Binyon continued his academic work: in May, 1939 he gave the prestigious Romanes Lecture in Oxford on Art and Freedom, and in 1940 he was appointed the Byron Professor of English Literature at the University of Athens. He worked there until forced to leave by the German invasion of Greece in April, 1941.

Binyon had been friends with Ezra Pound for a long time, and in the 1930s the two became especially close; Pound affectionately called him "BinBin", and he assisted Binyon with his translation of Dante.

Between 1933 and 1943, Binyon published his acclaimed translation of Dante's Divine Comedy in an English version of terza rima, made with some editorial assistance by Ezra Pound. It was acknowledged for many decades as the popular translation for Dante readers.

During the horrors of the Second World War Binyon wrote a poem that many claim as to be a masterpiece 'The Burning of the Leaves', puts in print his lines on the London Blitz.

At his death Binyon was working on a major three-part Arthurian trilogy, the first part of which was published after his death as The Madness of Merlin (1947).

Robert Laurence Binyon died in Dunedin Nursing Home, Bath Road, Reading, on March 10th, 1943 after undergoing an operation. A funeral service was held at Trinity College Chapel, Oxford, on March 13th, 1943.

Binyon's ashes were scattered at St. Mary's Church, Aldworth.

On November 11th, 1985, Binyon was among sixteen poets of the Great War commemorated on a slate stone unveiled in Westminster Abbey's Poets' Corner. The inscription on the stone quotes a fellow Great War poet, Wilfred Owen. It reads: "My subject is War, and the pity of War. The Poetry is in the pity."

Laurence Binyon – A Concise Bibliography

Poems and Verse
Persephone (1890)
Lyric Poems (1894)
The Praise of Life (1896)
Porphyrion & Other Poems (1898)
Odes (1901)
Death of Adam & Other Poems (1904)
Penthesilea (1905)
London Visions (1908)
England & Other Poems (1909)
Auguries (1913)
For The Fallen (The Times, September 21st, 1914)
The Winnowing Fan (1914)
The Anvil (1916)
The Cause (1917)
The New World: Poems (1918)
The Secret: Sixty Poems (1920)
The Idols (1928)
Collected Poems Vol I: London Visions, Narrative Poems, Translations (1931)
Collected Poems Vol II: Lyrical Poems (1931)
The North Star & Other Poems (1941)
The Burning of the Leaves & Other Poems (1944)
The Madness of Merlin (1947)

Poems Set to Music
In 1915 Cyril Rootham set "For the Fallen" for chorus and orchestra, first performed in 1919 by the Cambridge University Musical Society conducted by the composer.

Edward Elgar set to music "The Fourth of August", "To Women", and "For the Fallen", as The Spirit of England, Op. 80, for tenor or soprano solo, chorus and orchestra (1917).

English Arts and Myth
Dutch Etchers of the Seventeenth Century (1895), Binyon's first book on painting
John Crone and John Sell Cotman (1897)
William Blake: Being all his Woodcuts Photographically Reproduced in Facsimile (1902)
English Poetry in its relation to painting and the other arts (1918)
Drawings and Engravings of William Blake (1922)
Arthur: A Tragedy (1923)
The Followers of William Blake (1925)
The Engraved Designs of William Blake (1926)
Landscape in English Art and Poetry (1931)
English Watercolours (1933)
Gerard Hopkins and his influence (1939)

Art and freedom. (The Romanes lecture, delivered 25 May 1939). Oxford: The Clarendon press, (1939)

Japanese and Persian Arts
Painting in the Far East (1908)
Japanese Art (1909)
Flight of the Dragon (1911)
The Court Painters of the Grand Moguls (1921)
Japanese Colour Prints (1923)
The Poems of Nizami (1928) (Translation)
Persian Miniature Painting (1933)
The Spirit of Man in Asian Art (1936)
Autobiography[edit]
For Dauntless France (1918) (War memoir)

Biography
Botticelli (1913)
Akbar (1932)

Stage Plays
Brief Candles A verse-drama about the decision of Richard III to dispatch his two nephews
Paris and Œnone. A Tragedy in One Act (1906)
Godstow Nunnery: Play
Boadicea; A Play in eight Scenes
Attila: A Tragedy in Four Acts (1907)
Ayuli: A Play in three Acts and an Epilogue
Sophro the Wise: A Play for Children
(Most of the above were written for John Masefield's theatre).